IMAGES
of England

BIRMINGHAM
TRANSPORT

IMAGES
of England

BIRMINGHAM
TRANSPORT

Compiled by
Keith Turner

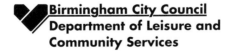

Birmingham City Council
Department of Leisure and
Community Services

TEMPUS

First published 1998, reprinted 2002

Tempus Publishing Limited
The Mill, Brimscombe Port,
Stroud, Gloucestershire, GL5 2QG

British Library Cataloguing in Publication Data.
A catalogue record for this book is available from the British Library.

ISBN 0 7524 1554 9

Typesetting and origination by Tempus Publishing Limited
Printed in Great Britain by Midway Colour Print, Wiltshire

Contents

Acknowledgements   6

Introduction   7

1.   Rural Rides   9

2.   Birmingham by Boat   19

3.   Buses, Coaches and Cabs   31

4.   Enter the Trams   47

5.   Railway Interlude   69

6.   Motoring for the Masses   77

7.   Commercial Haulage   89

8.   Flying High   99

9.   Miscellanea   115

Acknowledgements

I should like to thank, firstly, my former colleagues in Birmingham Central Library for showing such forebearance in the face of the disruption occasioned during the compilation of this book and, secondly, Andy Maxam and Jan Dobrzynski for providing technical details for some of the captions. Special thanks must also go to all historians of transport, from Birmingham and further afield, and all the local photographers whose prints are gathered in the library; without their earlier endeavours this compilation would never have been possible.

Introduction

Birmingham has long occupied a unique position at the very heart of England's transport networks. Sited in the geographical heart of the country, it quickly established itself in the late eighteenth century as the focal point of England's growing canal system, then half a century later did the same in terms of the newly invented railway. As metalled road building came into its own during the first half of the twentieth century, fuelled by the explosion in the number of motor vehicles using them, so the city became the natural hub of this network as well.

Within the city itself (or, before 1889, the town), Birmingham's residents could enjoy a wide variety of transport modes to help them on their way to work, to shops and markets, to theatres (and later to cinemas). Alternatively, on a Sunday or Bank Holiday, they could escape from the grime and heat of the streets into the surrounding countryside.

In providing transport for its citizens, Birmingham has always lived up to its 'Forward' motto and was at the forefront of each successive urban transport revolution: horse buses, steam and battery trams, overhead electric trams, suburban railway services and motor buses. All have had their heyday, but only the last two survive – although, at the time of writing, overhead electric trams are about to make a comeback in the shape of the new, state of the art Midland Metro which will link the city with West Bromwich and Wolverhampton.

Non-public aspects of the city's transport should not be forgotten. Birmingham has been frequently derided as being Britain's 'Motor City', an epithet based not only on the planning excesses of the 1960s and '70s, when great swathes of the city were razed to make way for new dual carriageways, but also on its long tradition of motorcar manufacture. The motor industry is still a major source of employment in Birmingham, although a more enlightened pedestrianization programme is now making the city centre a far more pleasant place for inhabitants and visitors alike.

The photographs in this book are very much a personal selection from those stored in Birmingham Central Library and include vehicles from all of the above mentioned modes of transport, as well as from agriculture, aviation, commercial haulage and those used in leisure activities. I hope they provide the true flavour of just one aspect of life in this great city.

Birmingham Cab Company, Limited.

GENERAL HIRING ESTABLISHMENT,
BRISTOL STREET DEPÔT.

HENRY J. HART, Manager.

Every Description of Private Carriages for Hire, also the Royal Forder Hansom Cabs by the Hour, Day, or Week.

SPECIAL VICTORIA HANSOMS,

And C Spring Cabs, for Private, Medical, or Commercial use.

GENTLEMEN'S CARRIAGE HORSES FOR HIRE,
Single or Pairs.

J. C. ROBINSON,
GENERAL MANAGER,
NEWHALL CHAMBERS, BIRMINGHAM.

An advertisement from Hart's *Coaching and Tourists' Guide of Warwickshire*, published in 1885. (Photographs of hansom cabs similar to that portrayed here can be seen on pp. 38-9.) Such adverts, and others for inns and hotels, were commonly found in travellers' guidebooks of the time.

One
Rural Rides

At the beginning of the nineteenth century, encompassed within what is now the modern Birmingham boundary, was a small manufacturing and market town surrounded by a number of self-contained villages, with their farms growing produce to feed the hungry workers of the industrial centre. With the subsequent growth of the town, village after village was slowly but surely incorporated into Birmingham's outer districts and suburbs until the area became a single urban mass with only the occasional park or common to provide relief from the relentless spread of houses, shops and factories. This opening selection of photographs reminds us just how rural much of the city once was – and how late in the century some parts of it remained so.

Two young boys enjoy a summer's day ride at the turn of the century, with their horse contentedly cooling its hooves in the River Cole at Hay Mills.

Heybarnes Farm on the Coventry Road in Hay Mills, c. 1900. A scene that would have been familiar to countless generations of the inhabitants of Birmingham's outskirts: the annual ritual of hay making.

Two Warstock Farm carts on the site of what is now Yardley Wood school, 1913. The farmhands are, from left to right: Frank Holt, Thomas Reeves, Ted Reeves and Tom Taylor. Each horse is sporting a hanging brass on its facepiece, while the two on the right have brasses on their nosebands.

A horse and tip-cart at Tritterford Farm, Hall Green, 1918. The cart is equipped with side boards, for transporting high loads, spades and a tarpaulin cover, while the horse is wearing its workaday harness with the brasswork confined to buckles and the square identification plates on the saddle.

Another wheeled tip-cart belonging to Thomas Reeves of Tritterford Farm in 1910. The cart was manufactured by Lewis' wheelwright's of Peterbrook Road, Shirley, and the horse is decked out for the May Day celebrations in its best harness with a full set of brasses on every available strip of leather.

The wheelwright's premises of E. Shephard, Wharf Road, King's Norton, 1897. Such businesses were as commonplace and indispensable as garages and car repair shops are today.

Another Tritterford Farm cart, although this is a lighter, more elegant vehicle made ready for the May Day festivities in 1913.

In contrast, this similar one-horse cart, belonging to William Florence of Hay Farm, Hay Mills, can be seen in normal everyday use at about the same time.

An assembly of living vans, as used by fairground folk, gathered on the village green at King's Norton for the annual Mop Fair, *c.* 1895.

A gypsy encampment on Black Patch common at Handsworth, around 1895. Although the caravans here are similar in size and wheel arrangement to those in the previous photograph, there are obvious differences in the bodywork favoured by the two sets of travellers.

Moseley was one of a string of semi-rural communities around the centre of Birmingham and this picture shows the heart of village, well before the 1890s, with traffic virtually non-existent.

A similar view to the one above, with evidence of considerable rebuilding on the left, *c.* 1895. Tramlines, which had by now been laid in the foreground, link the village with Birmingham, as might the assorted horse cabs waiting for fares by the new cabmen's shelter.

Tritterford Farm in May 1919. Thomas Reeves takes a break from ploughing to pose proudly on his farm's first tractor: a Fordson Model F, the tractor that did more than any other to revolutionize agricultural practices in the twentieth century. Nearly three-quarters of a million of them were built between 1917 and 1928. British models were built at Dagenham, although the slots on the side of the radiator indicate that this particular vehicle is a 1917 American export.

The traditional horse and cart did not disappear from Birmingham's farms and highways overnight, as proved by the sight of this one in service at King's Farm in Gospel Lane, Acock's Green, in 1920 ...

... and two more in Longbridge Lane, Longbridge, in 1932 ...

... and one in Moor Green Lane, Moseley, also in 1932. Their use would receive a temporary respite during the Second World War, before finally succumbing to the inexorable advance of the internal combustion engine.

When motor transport took over, the resulting heavier loads carried on speedier vehicles meant that roadways had to be upgraded drastically. Not everything could be done at once, of course, as illustrated by the hazard presented to motorists by this ford on the River Cole in Lea Ford Road, Kitt's Green, in May 1938.

Some twenty years later a similar obstacle still survived on the River Cole, this time in Scribers Lane, Yardley Wood – this is an obstacle which a shire horse would have taken in its stride!

Two

Birmingham by Boat

The first English canals of the Industrial Revolution were dug in the 1750s and by the end of the century virtually the whole of a 4,000 mile network of these artificial waterways was in place. They were constructed by the itinerant gangs of labourers known as 'navigators' – a name soon shortened to the more familiar 'navvies' – and linked the sources of raw materials and fuel with the great new factories of the age. These manufacturing centres were in turn linked with their major markets in the towns and cities of England. The Industrial Revolution may have made the goods, but the canals most certainly made the Industrial Revolution, stretching as they did from the Thames to the Severn, the Mersey, the Trent and the Humber, with Birmingham at their centre.

This timeless scene was once commonplace on English canals when they were still freight highways of importance rather than leisure playgrounds. Here the narrowboat *Frampton*, belonging to the Severn & Canal Carrying Co. Ltd, earns its keep on the Worcester & Birmingham Canal near Selly Oak on 11 June 1936.

The canal wharf at Lifford, looking towards Bredon Bridge on the Pershore Road, in the 1900s. Two working barges can be seen with members of their crews and railway yard staff. The coal trucks in the background would have been brought by rail from the collieries and their contents loaded into barges at wharves like this up and down the country. Delivery could then be made directly into canalside factories. The man holding the horse, beside the railway box vans on the left, is thought to be Mr J. Wilkes whilst the gentleman at the tiller of his barge is Joseph Millard of Stirchley. Both men are wearing 'billycocks' – hard felt hats favoured by a certain class of worker to denote their status as being above that of a common labourer.

Members of King's Norton Baptist church on an outing standing by the Stratford-on-Avon Canal's No. 1 Lock at King's Norton, *c.* 1912. To the left is one of the lock's pair of guillotine gates, unique in this country, where the canal joins the Worcester & Birmingham Canal. The canal was begun in 1793, was virtually derelict by the 1950s, but was restored and reopened in 1964, one of the first great successes of the modern canal restoration movement.

Just east of King's Norton is the King's Norton (or Brandwood) Tunnel, *c.* 1910. The tunnel was 352 yds long and 16 ft wide which meant that, unlike many other canal tunnels, two narrowboats could just pass each other inside it. The two niches in the brickwork of the portal were apparently intended to house a pair of statues.

Salford Junction in 1913. Here, at Gravelly Hill, the Birmingham & Fazeley Canal from Gas Street Basin met the Tame Valley Canal from Perry Barr. Manual dredging is taking place for, as on all artificial waterways, maintenance was an ongoing task.

This damaged bridge, which carried Alcester Road South over the Stratford-on-Avon Canal, is being inspected and photographed on 28 July 1938. Unlike road bridges, canal bridges posed special problems of access when repairs were called for.

Another repair job in the offing in 1906. Here, the Birmingham & Fazeley Canal has burst its bank in the city centre and, no longer watertight, has simply drained a whole section of the waterway.

This may look like a similar scene but is in fact a terminal branch of the Birmingham Canal, complete with lock gates, which was unearthed near the end of Broad Street during excavations for the city's new civic centre in 1936. The canal reached the town from Wednesbury in 1769. The domed structure in the background is the Hall of Memory, opened in 1925.

The Canal Navigation Office of the Birmingham Canal in 1907. This impressive structure in Paradise Street was built in 1771 and demolished in 1928. Judging by the flags, the carefully posed carts and the assembled officials, the occasion was a very special one indeed. Behind the office was the Old Wharf where cargoes could be transhipped right in the heart of the city at the end of a short canal branch from Gas Street Basin.

The rear of the Birmingham Canal Office, *c.* 1935. The large canal basins were later filled in and the whole site levelled in the 1960s to make way for the ATV House complex. The cargo in evidence here appears to be either stone or washed coal.

The same wharf looking towards the council house with its distinctive clock tower across a hive of activity. They are transhipping what appears to be coal (or possibly stone!) again. The date of this picture is sometime before the demolition of Christ Church at the top of New Street in 1899, the spire of which can be seen on the right.

The Old Wharf in 1913, full of boats and coal ...

... and again in the 1930s, now deserted and derelict prior to being filled in.

Farmer's Bridge Locks on the Birmingham & Fazeley Canal in 1913. This single flight contains no less than thirteen locks in succession. The horse was still a prime mover on the inland waterways, although it was in competition with steam and internal combustion engines.

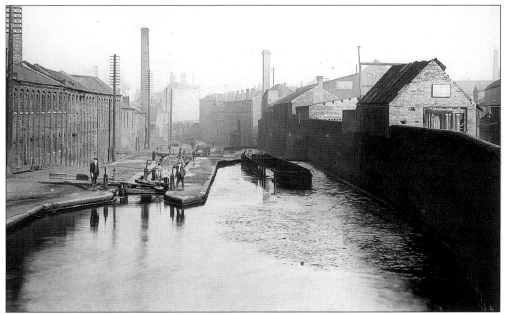

The same locks in 1913, this time seen from higher up the flight.

The upper entrance to the same flight of locks, some forty years on, when commercial traffic had all but vanished. Behind the camera is Farmer's Bridge Junction where this canal from Salford Junction and the ones going north to Wolverhampton and south to Worcester or Stratford meet.

In complete contrast, the same scene can be seen another twenty years on in the early 1970s. The derelict industrial site on the right has been cleared, high-rise flats have been built behind Cambrian Wharf, a canalside walk has been laid out and the whole area has been generally smartened up in time for the 1969 bicentenary celebration of the opening of the Birmingham Canal.

Like any other craft, canal boats had to be built and maintained. This is the Saltley Dock premises of the firm of Morton, Fellows & Clayton with the *Egypt* in the foreground nearing completion; it left the yard on 18 December 1903. Working on her are, from left to right: R.A. Osborne, J.W. Gold, -?-, -?- and Tom Cox.

Gas Street Basin in 1958. After the working boats left the canal, residential and hire boats moved in slowly taking up the vacant berths in the shadow of the empty warehouses where the Birmingham Canal Navigations, on the left, met the Worcester & Birmingham Canal. Directly ahead, beyond the appropriately named Bridge Street, is the filled in Old Wharf.

The same scene twenty years on, on 9 March 1978, with local schoolchildren inspecting the basin as it undergoes a major transformation. In the centre foreground is the future site of the James Brindley public house and behind it, ATV House and Alpha Tower. The narrow stretch of water in the foreground once housed a bar of a very different kind, used to prevent boats from passing through to the neighbouring waterway system; instead, cargoes had to manhandled over it from one boat to another! The last twenty years have seen even greater changes with the redevelopment of the entire Broad Street area.

Three
Buses, Coaches and Cabs

The very first horse bus service in Birmingham is thought to have been that operated by Mr John Smith of the Malt Shovel Inn, Smallbrook Street. It ran four times a day from the Swan in Snow Hill via Bull Street, the High Street and Smallbrook Street, then down the Bristol Road as far as the first turnpike gate. After that, the idea of such vehicles slowly spread and by the end of the century a number of operators – including Birmingham's horse tramway companies – had several hundred of them on the city's streets. The first motor buses appeared early in the next century and, on 1 June 1905, the Birmingham & Midland Motor Omnibus Co. Ltd began operating fifteen 'Red' double-deckers (as well as scores of horse buses). The next major player on the scene was the Corporation which began services on 19 July 1913, with ten Daimler 10 hp vehicles in a blue and cream livery. The Corporation operated a service to Rednal from its Selly Oak tram terminus and from these small beginnings, a great fleet was to grow.

Birmingham's heart: the Bull Ring, with the statue of Lord Nelson and St Martin's church in the centre, c. 1840. This was a major departure point for stage coaches such as those seen in this print; the notice on the building to the right advertises their services.

HEN AND CHICKENS
𝔥𝔬𝔱𝔢𝔩,

NEW-STREET, BIRMINGHAM.

ROYAL MAILS & *FAST* POST COACHES
TO EVERY TOWN IN THE KINGDOM.

Amongst the numerous celebrated conveyances from this Office, will be found

The Oxford Day,..	at ¼ before 12, A.M.
The Courier, ...	½ past 7, ——
The Tantivy, to Oxford and London,	at ½ past 8, A.M.
The last Royal Mail, to London, ..	½ past 11, P.M.
The Royal Mail, to Sheffield, ...	½ past 5, A.M.
The Telegraph, to Sheffield and Leeds, ..	½ past 8, ——
The Mercury, to Bath	½ past 8, ——
The Alert, to Cheltenham	½ past 2, P.M.
The Erin Go Bragh, to Oxford and London,	8, ——
The Royal Mail, to Bath and Exeter, ..	8, ——

Persons leaving Manchester and Liverpool by the last Train, and taking this conveyance from Birmingham, will reach London in 15 hours.

HEN AND CHICKENS HOTEL,
NEW-STREET, BIRMINGHAM.

The Post Horses belonging to this Establishment are *First-Rate*, and are in constant readiness upon the arrival of the Trains at the Railway Station.

An advertisement from *The Grand Junction Railway Companion*, 1837, published in Birmingham, Liverpool and London. It is representative of that brief period of English transport history when the stage coach (so named because it travelled stage by stage, changing horses along the way) and the railway operated side by side – or, more accurately, end to end.

A stage coach outside the Stork Hotel in the Old Square, *c.* 1865. Its long-distance travelling days were numbered by the spreading railway network; the coaching inn, however, adapted easily as the trains brought greater numbers of visitors to the city. The novelty of the camera has ensured a good crowd of onlookers in the background.

A horse bus in New Street in 1868. Like the stage coach, it too would be replaced with its passengers being captured by the development of suburban rail services, the coming tramways and eventually the motor bus.

A horse bus makes a leisurely stop by the Mermaid Inn in the Stratford Road for local photographer Thomas Lewis in 1873. Although vastly altered, this location at the junction with the Warwick Road in Sparkhill is paradoxically easily recognizable today. The two-tone livery of the bus is readily apparent, as is the longitudinal seat employed to save weight on the ridge of the lower saloon's turtle-roof and the 'decency boards' fitted to shield the legs of female passengers travelling on top (or 'outside' in stage coach parlance) from prying eyes. This road would normally have been busy with agricultural and other traffic, so presumably the photographer waited for a quiet moment to take his long-exposure picture.

A heavily retouched but rare photograph of a horse bus yard and blacksmith's forge in Handsworth in 1871. The buses might well have been constructed here, or at a local wheelwright's premises, although manufacturers in London, Birkenhead and elsewhere were beginning to supply the national market.

These two horse buses in Station Street are apparently awaiting passengers for the journey to Balsall Heath, c. 1890; the fare was 1d all the way. The tramway tracks just visible in the shadow in the foreground presage the end of the road for these vehicles.

Another superb Thomas Lewis photograph, this time a famous view of New Street, *c*. 1890. The camera is looking down from the town hall past the post office (opened in 1890) and the statue of Sir Robert Peel towards New Street railway station. Christ Church is on the far left. The 1d horse bus in the foreground has just travelled the length of Broad Street from Five Ways; its conductor is standing with his cash bag on the rear platform. The large, different sized front and rear wheels mounted outside the vehicle's body are a direct legacy from the stage coach which would be abandoned by the tramcar.

A very late horse bus survivor was this Hagley Road service to Bearwood, seen here arriving in Victoria Square, *c.* 1910. Its upper deck passengers are elegantly behatted as fashion and etiquette then decreed.

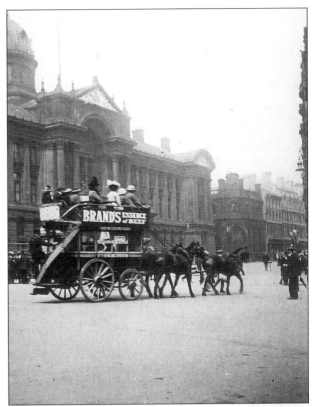

Another late-surviving service was the one that ran along the Stratford Road. A two-horse double-decker follows the tramlines through Sparkbrook, *c.* 1912. The word 'bus' came into being as an abbreviation of 'omnibus', Latin for 'for everyone' – although not everyone wished to ride on such 'lower class' vehicles.

For those not willing to mix with *hoi polloi* on an omnibus, or whose journey necessitated it, there was always the hansom cab, named after its architect designer Joseph Aloysius Hansom (who also designed the town hall). Here one waits for a fare in Station Street in 1892. Note the driver's high but exposed driving position and the folding doors to help shield his passengers.

The Mermaid Hotel on the Stratford Road again, around the time it was rebuilt (1895). Two hansom cabs – one of which appears to be lacking a horse – flank a larger brougham in front of the cabmen's shelter.

A hansom cab at Five Ways after a severe storm in February 1909. The exposed driving position is clearly visible, as is the vehicle's licence plate (No. 458) and the large bag of horse feed hanging from the roof. The horse munches patiently from its nosebag as the driver shelters somewhere out of the cold.

In complete contrast, Five Ways in the motor bus age just eleven years later. This Tilling-Stevens TTA2 double-decker O9914, built in 1912, was bought from the BMMO by the Corporation in 1914 and is waiting outside Lloyds Bank, out of service, beside an array of petrol cans while a Corporation Daimler sails by on its Route 1 journey from Moseley.

A horse-drawn charabanc outside the Plumbers Arms in King's Norton, *c*. 1912. These lofty vehicles, requiring a team of horses to pull them when full, were in great demand for group outings of all kinds – temperance or otherwise – in the years prior to the outbreak of the First World War. The nature of this gentlemen-only excursion, given the location, is probably 'otherwise'! The name 'charabanc' is derived from the French for 'carriage with benches'.

Another gentlemen's outing from a King's Norton hostelry, this time the Saracens Head, in the 1920s. After the First World War, the horse-drawn 'chara' gave way to the internal combustion engined variety. This was basically a large, elongated motorcar with or without a rudimentary roof.

Gravelley Hill in 1924. Midland Red's Tilling-Stevens TS3 single-decker OE1137, built in 1919, leads a Corporation double-decker tramcar over Salford Bridge on its Birmingham to Streetly service. Corporation buses were restricted to operations within the city boundary while the BMMO Midland Red served the villages and towns beyond.

Erdington High Street in April 1928. Here, a brand-new Corporation ADC507 follows tram No. 696 (built by Brush in 1925) on its Route 17 journey between the Maypole and Erdington via the city centre. This service had been inaugurated only the month before.

664

TRAVEL
by
Midland
"RED."

REGULAR AND RELIABLE SERVICES TO AND FROM BIRMINGHAM AND

STRATFORD,	WARWICK,	EVESHAM,
COVENTRY,	LEAMINGTON,	KENILWORTH,
STOURBRIDGE,	KIDDERMINSTER,	MALVERN,
BRIERLEY HILL,	DUDLEY,	WOLVERHAMPTON,
		etc.

THROUGH DAILY SERVICES TO—

LEICESTER,	NORTHAMPTON,	LOUGHBOROUGH,
WORCESTER,	NOTTINGHAM,	WOLVERHAMPTON,
	WESTON-SUPER-MARE.	

SAVE 2d. IN THE 1/-

On your Ordinary 'Bus Fares by using Books of Discount Tickets. Sold by Midland **"RED"** Inspectors and at Company's Offices and Agencies.

N.B.—Not available on Seaside Services.

5/- "ANYWHERE" TICKETS, 5/-

Have a Day sight-seeing all over the Midland " **RED** " Country for **5/-**

Travel on any Ordinary Service 'Bus on Day of Issue and Change Vehicles and Routes as often as desired.

Available Tuesdays, Wednesdays, Thursdays, and Fridays

Sold at Company's Offices and Agencies. Not available on Limited Stop Services.

CHIEF OFFICES :—	MIDLAND " RED " TRAVEL BUREAU :—
BEARWOOD, BIRMINGHAM.	BULL RING, BIRMINGHAM
Tel. : Bearwood 2020.	Tel. : Midland 3887.

O. C. POWER, TRAFFIC MANAGER.

The inside cover advertisement of the Midland Red's 1929 A to Z pocket timetable, listing places served and special tickets available. The bus illustrated is a 1929 type Q (for Queen) single-decker.

A Corporation-owned Daimler COG5 single-decker BOL34, built in 1936, makes its unhindered way along Route 27, Hay Green to King's Heath via Bournville, some time prior to its 1950 withdrawal. This bus, along with other members of its class, was used as an ambulance during 1939 and 1940. Its bodywork was made by Metro-Cammell in Birmingham.

A Corporation-owned bus, FOF143, in Pershore Road South in 1950. It is a 1939 double-decker version of the Daimler COG5 seen in the previous photograph. The bus – again unencumbered by other traffic – is on Service 18A, King's Norton to Yardley Wood Road via Northfield, and was withdrawn the following year.

The successor to the charabanc was the enclosed single-decker coach as built by a number of manufacturers and supplied to hire companies. This Yardley Coaches vehicle is on hire to Mr W. Meddings of Hay Mills, seen left with his son, probably during the late 1940s or early '50s.

Trolleybuses began operating in Birmingham under Corporation ownership in 1922 and lasted until 1951. They worked principally down the Coventry Road and travelled to various destinations. Here, trolleybus OC1131 is seen in Birmingham High Street near Martineau Street on Service 94, to the city boundary.

Trolleybus OC1128 on Service 94 in 1951, this time at the Coventry Road terminus. Note the double wire overhead, as distinct to the single wire used by trams, and the Bundy clock on the pavement for drivers to key into, to record their punctual (or otherwise) departure.

Trolleybus OC1136 in service on the Coventry Road again in 1951. Like its fellow vehicles, OC1131 and OC1128 in the previous two photographs, this vehicle was built by Leyland in 1934 as a type TTBD2 with Metro-Cammell bodywork.

The former Midland Red bus station, 1967, four years after it opened as part of the new Bull Ring shopping centre. It was ideally sited, close to the markets and New Street railway station. Buses entered the station here from Dudley Street and exited via Edgbaston Street, passing under the new Smallbrook Queensway dual carriageway while inside.

The bus station interior, 1967, with a variety of Midland Red buses waiting to depart. Despite its prime site, the station rapidly became a dismal and unattractive place and has been the subject of relocation plans and proposals for many years.

Four

Enter the Trams

Birmingham's tramway system – with over 80 miles of route, one of the largest in the country – operated for virtually the whole life span of this mode of transport as an urban mass-mover. Because of its longevity, it employed, during its lifetime, all the main tramway traction methods including horse power, steam haulage and overhead electric current, as well as two lesser ones: cable haulage and battery-electric power. The town's first line to be opened (worked by horses) was from West Bromwich across the boundary at Hockley Brook in 1872; the last were electric routes closed in 1953, making the system one of the last in England to be abandoned (see pp. 67-8). Its late demise means that many of the city's older residents have vivid memories of the blue and cream double-deckers that once served them so well.

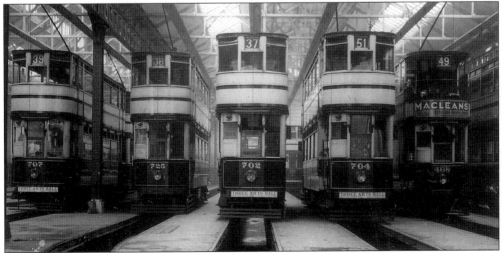

Trafalgar Road tram depot in Moseley with tramcars, from left to right: Nos 707, 725, 702 and 704, built by Brush in 1925–26, and No. 408, built by Dick, Kerr in 1912.

THE LAST HORSE TRAM (NECHELLS.)
SEPT 30/06
PHOTO BY A TWIGG BLOOMSBURY ST

Birmingham's last horse tram on the Albert Street to Nechells route on 30 September 1906, the day such workings ceased in the city. The tramcar is an unidentified City of Birmingham Tramways double-decker, of which the company owned ten. By this date, most British horse tramway systems had closed, usually being rebuilt as electric tramways (as in this case), and this would have been a rare survivor, its design typical of such vehicles built twenty years before. Note the subtle differences in dress between the driver and his conductor to denote the difference in status. The issuing of commercial postcards such as this one often commemorated these historic moments.

A similar tramcar on the Nechells route also in 1906; this time the driver is less formally attired.

A Birmingham Central Tramway steam tram and trailer No. 45, in Moat Road in the late 1880s. The tram is on Service S, to Sparkbrook. The company owned 102 locomotives and 76 double-decker trailers. No. 45 was a Falcon product built in 1885–86.

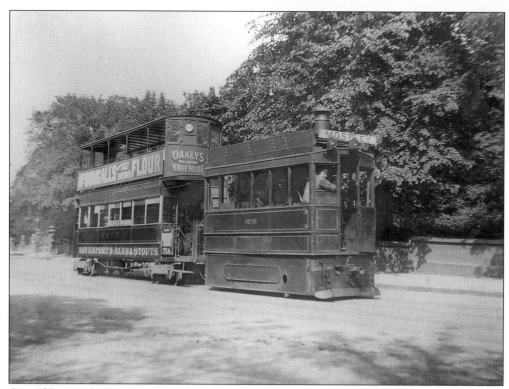

City of Birmingham Tramways steam tram No. 38 (a Falcon, built in 1885), with trailer in the Alcester Road on Service M to Moseley in 1906. The distinctive features of the locomotive with its motion enclosed to meet the Board of Trade's safety requirements and the trailer are readily apparent. The superior pulling power of a steam locomotive meant that a longer, eight-wheeled trailer could be hauled, which in turn meant that more passengers could be carried per trip than by a horse car. The increased pulling power also made a roof to the trailer's upper deck possible, so increasing passenger comfort. The City of Birmingham Tramways Co. Ltd took over the Birmingham Central Tramway Co. Ltd in 1896.

A CBT tram locomotive (possibly No. 78, a Kitson product built in the late 1890s) and trailer on Service K to King's Heath in 1906.

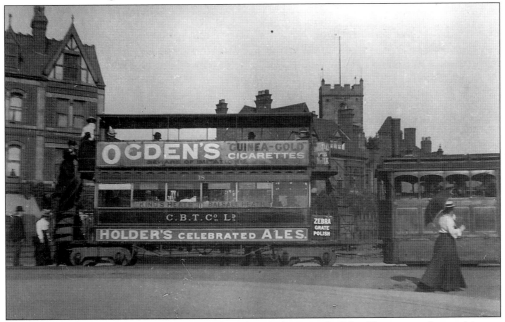

Moseley village in 1902, with passengers boarding Falcon trailer No. 18 on a similar working to that in the photograph above. Judging by the passengers' dress, and the parasol carried by the lady on the right, it would seem to be sometime in the high summer.

Another CBT steam tram and trailer on the Sparkbrook route in 1905. The location is the Stratford Road junction with Farm Road in Sparkbrook. The work gang appears to be digging up the roadway prior to laying a second line of track ready for the Corporation's electric tramcars.

A similar service in the depths of winter in 1906. The location is the Stratford Road, near its junction with Ladypool Road.

The old offices of the (officially titled) Birmingham Central Tramway Co. Ltd in Old Square, looking down towards the Law Courts and Central Hall, 1890s. This building was the last surviving structure in Lichfield Street before it was cleared and redeveloped to become the lower end of Corporation Street. The group of people on the right are waiting for a tramcar at the terminus.

Birmingham briefly saw the use of battery-electric trams on the BCT's line from Suffolk Street down the Bristol Road to Bournbrook. Formerly a standard gauge horse tramway, it was worked by the new tramcars, from 24 July 1890 until 14 May 1901, on the 3 ft 6 inch gauge common to Birmingham and the Black Country. Here, tramcar No. 102 waits in Suffolk Street at the turn of the century.

Birmingham was one of a handful of locations in Britain that could boast a cable tramway, worked by a continually moving cable in a conduit between the rails to which a tramcar could be attached by driver-controlled grippers. This system was employed principally to climb steep hills. In Birmingham, a line of this type was opened from the Grand Hotel in Colmore Row to Hockley Brook from 24 March 1888, and was extended to the New Inns, Handsworth, on 20 April 1888. It was replaced by Corporation electric trams on 1 July 1911. Here the crew and passers-by pose for the camera by tramcar No. 81 outside the appropriately-named Cable Tramway Inn in Hockley Brook in July 1890. The spur in the foreground led to the depot for the line's ten single-decker and thirty-eight double-decker tramcars.

A cable car in Snow Hill passes the Great Western Railway's station of that name, shortly after commencing its journey to Handsworth in 1900. The scene is unrecognizable today, save for the fact that a new station occupies the same site on the left.

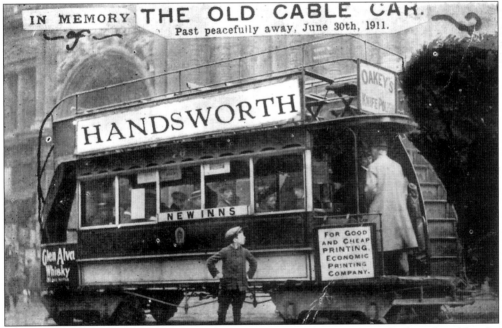

The last day of cable working, as recorded by this commemorative postcard produced by the Economic Printing Co. of 54 Pershore Street. (Note the publisher's advertisement superimposed on the tram!)

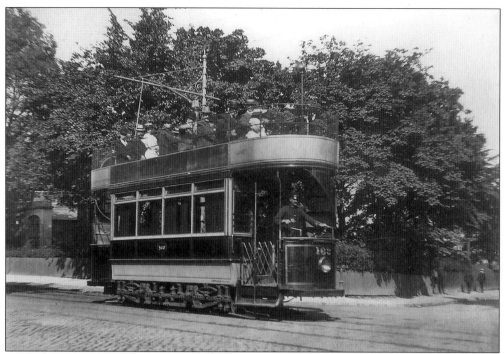

Corporation tramcar No. 163, a United Electric Car Co. product built in 1906, in Balsall Heath. It is seen here on the first day of the new electric tramcar service along the Moseley Road to King's Heath on 1 January 1907. The tramcar appears to be sporting curtains in the lower deck saloon, possibly for the benefit of an official party.

The same route, this time in Moseley village looking towards Birmingham, possibly also in 1907. Tramcar No. 91, a sister car to that in the photograph above, is departing.

A postcard of a Corporation open-top tramcar, decorated and illuminated for the visit of King Edward VII and Queen Alexandra to open the University of Birmingham on 7 July 1909. Such extravagant displays were common expressions of civic pride in the pre-First World War years...

... and on this occasion even included tram shelters, as in the case of this one, bedecked to resemble a tramcar. The trams' predecessors, horse buses, picked up and set down passengers anywhere along their route whereas tramcars required fixed stops, an idea later adopted by the motor buses.

An early view of the Highgate Road depot in the electric era. Tramcars No. 8 (built by the Electric Railway & Tramway Carriage Works in 1904 and fitted with a top cover in 1905) and No. 31 (built by DK in 1905) are identifiable on the left behind the inspection pits. The travelling crane is lifting a motor, possibly from the truck in the left foreground.

Postcards were often issued by local publishers to record tramway mishaps. This one, produced by Edwards & Co. of New Street, shows the aftermath of a fatal derailment in Warstone Lane on 1 October 1907. DK tramcar, No. 22 of 1905 is being righted with the aid of the wooden gantry erected on the left.

Inevitably, the tramways were seriously affected by the bombings of the Second World War. Tracks were wrecked and, as here at Miller Street off New Town Row, depots and tramcars were damaged and destroyed.

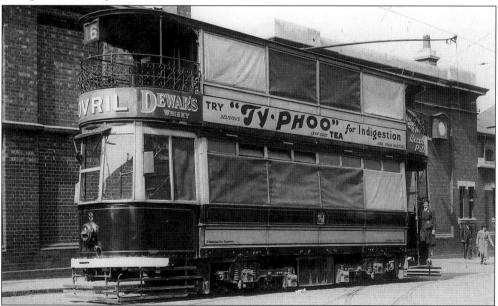

Many tramcars did make it through the war years unscathed, however. Here, ERTC No. 3 shows off its new wartime look, complete with blackout blinds and masked headlamps, c. 1939. As elsewhere in the country, female 'clippies' were a common sight, replacing men called up for military service.

Central Place in Gosta Green on a snowy day in the early 1930s. A number of tramway routes met on this approach into the city centre. A white-coated policeman directs traffic on the left while horse carts are in evidence on the right.

An identical view in September 1937, with the new fire station in pride of place. The road layout and tram tracks have been remodelled slightly and two trolleybuses have made an appearance with OJ1012 (a type 663T built by AEC in 1932), on the Nechells route to the fore. This vehicle was withdrawn in 1940 when the service was discontinued. Also in the foreground is tram No. 668 (built in 1924), with No. 337 (built in 1911) in the distance.

Central Place – now renamed Lancaster Place – in 1950. Brush-built tramcars Nos 686 and 700 (built in 1924–25) are passing on Service 79, Steelhouse Lane to Pype Hayes and Service 2, Steelhouse Lane to Erdington.

On 25 September 1938 a new reserved track line running along Sutton New Road was opened by the Corporation to bypass the older section in Erdington High Street. Here, workmen are engaged in making the connection between the new and old routes just two days before. Note the tower wagon in the distance used when stringing the overhead wire and the tie-rods which held the grooved rails to gauge.

The Bristol Road route to the city boundary at Rednal and Rubery was one of the showpieces of Birmingham's tramway system. Here, track is being laid on the southwards extension from Selly Oak at the top of Pigeon House Hill in Northfield on 24 September 1923. Because the line was being laid beside rather than in the roadway, ballasted tracks were used with the rails fastened to sleepers as on a railway. (Compare this with the previous photograph.)

Looking up Pigeon House Hill from the other side on the same day. Hawkesley Mill Lane is off to the right. Steamroller OK8263 stands by the temporary railhead.

This is a similar scene, six months later, by Tessall Farm in Northfield looking towards the city on 5 March 1924. The overhead wires are now up, the track is ballasted, and an ALL CARS STOP HERE sign erected to the left of the houses.

With very few exceptions, the Bristol Road routes ran entirely on reserved track to ensure traffic-free travelling. One of the exceptions was the bridge over the railway siding into the Longbridge car works, seen here on 18 May 1925. Work is underway to lay the final section of one of the two tramway tracks, the other already being used on the other side of the fencing down the middle of the road.

Bristol Road, Edgbaston, *c.* 1930. Tramcar No. 391 (built by DK in 1912) on Service 71, Navigation Street to Rubery, passes two horse-drawn delivery vans on the left, two delivery boys on bicycles on the right and a handful of assorted motor vehicles to give a perfect example of the 'grand vistas' afforded by this route.

Griffins Hill on the Selly Oak boundary in 1944. Tramcars Nos 587 and 589 (Brush-built vehicles from 1920), have just passed each other. The shuttered headlamps and the lack of motor traffic on the road are telling indications that the country was still at war.

In contrast, the bustle of Steelhouse Lane terminus in the city centre on 4 July 1952. Tramcar No. 642 was one of a class of twenty-five cars supplied by the Birmingham firm of Midland Railway Carriage & Wagon Co. Ltd in 1923. It can be seen working Service 78, to Short Heath, and is about to be overtaken by a Midland Red double-decker outside the Wesleyan & General Assurance building.

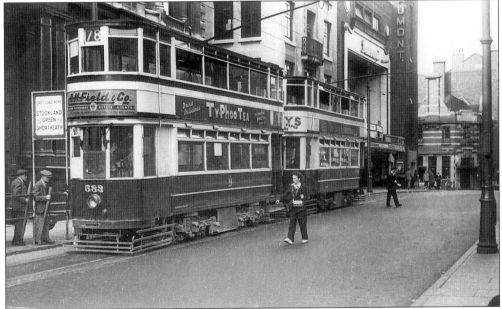

Steelhouse Lane again, looking the other way past the Gaumont cinema with tramcar No. 583 (built by UEC in 1914) on Service 78 and a similar class tramcar possibly on Service 2 to Erdington. Their conductress and conductor are both reversing the trolley poles prior to departure while keeping a lookout for approaching traffic.

Football specials were very much a feature of urban tramways. Here, at least seventeen cars wait in Garrison Lane near Birmingham City's ground on 24 September 1938 to take spectators – and in those days, players as well! – to their homes.

Birmingham's most modern tramcar was No. 843, seen here on an enthusiasts' special charter making a round trip across the Birmingham and Black Country linked systems. This tramcar was built at the Cotteridge depot (with a Brush body) in 1930 and ran for 432,500 miles before being withdrawn and scrapped in August 1952.

The last trams ran in Birmingham on the Short Heath, Pype Hayes and Erdington routes on 4 July 1953. Here tramcar No. 623 (Brush-built in 1920) leaves the Miller Street depot on that day, with Transport Department employees aboard taking a final trip.

This was one of the last day's trams at the Erdington terminus and is seen with large crowds hoping for one last ride.

Tramcar No. 616 (Brush-built in 1920) was Birmingham's official 'last tram' and halted here in Sutton Road before moving on to the Erdington terminus for the very last time. Among the dignitaries aboard was the Lord Mayor, Alderman G.H.W. Griffith, seen here on No. 616's platform. Once the occasion was over, No. 616 was broken up at Witton depot after more than thirty years' faithful service.

Five

Railway Interlude

The Railway Age came early to Birmingham when the Grand Junction Railway arrived at a temporary terminus at Vauxhall by Erskine Street Bridge, opened on 4 July 1837; a permanent terminus in Curzon Street followed two years later. After that, other companies arrived thick and fast to Birmingham. After a period of amalgamation, two principal operators emerged. They were the London & North Western Railway (part of the London, Midland & Scottish Railway from 1923) with a main line from New Street to London Euston, and the Great Western Railway with a main line from Snow Hill to London Paddington. With other routes radiating to all parts of the country, Birmingham was established as the hub of a regional railway network, a position it holds to this day. Many photographs of the city's railways have been published over the years; in this selection I have tried to give a sample of its multiple facets in the space available.

Photographs of railway construction are necessarily rare, as the bulk of it took place before the era of photography. This commercial postcard shows, in the background, the rural idyll of Sarehole being shattered by the construction of the GWR's North Warwickshire line in the early 1900s.

A closer view of the construction of the North Warwickshire line, 1906, although the exact location is unknown. A contractor's saddle tank locomotive is hauling away a rake of trucks, presumably loaded with spoil from the cutting under construction. The line, which was independently promoted, was taken over by the GWR before construction began and opened to take passengers from Tyseley to Stratford on 1 July 1908.

A new railway station was constructed at Lea Hall to serve the housing development there in May 1938. The station, on the LMS's main line from New Street to London, was opened on 1 May 1939 and is still very much used by commuters into central Birmingham.

The LMS's Harborne railway station in 1934, shortly before it closed to passengers on 24 November that year. An ex-LNWR 0-6-2 tank engine prepares to depart with a goods train of LMS and private wagons. This short branch, off the New Street – Wolverhampton main line, was just 2½ miles long and opened on 10 August 1874, closing on 2 November 1963. Much of the trackbed was made into a walkway in 1981.

A contractor's railway of a very different kind: drainage work beside the Pershore Road in King's Norton in 1924. This was still the era of manual labour and the two skip wagons visible would have been pushed by hand along the lightly laid narrow gauge track.

Snow Hill railway station on 30 May 1955. A national rail strike in May 1955 hit services all over the country although a skeleton service of sorts operated wherever possible. Here, one of the station's staff writes out the daily notice advising hopeful passengers exactly what they could expect. The station closed on 6 March 1972, with demolition work already begun.

The ornate wrought-iron work over the side entrance to the booking hall at Snow Hill with the GWR's monogram in the centre, designed so that it could be read from both sides. It was rescued during further demolition work in 1977 and is now displayed in the foyer of the modern office building erected on the site.

Snow Hill railway station, 1965. A former GWR tank engine, 4555, a regular sight at Snow Hill, passed through on a goods train. Built in 1924, 4555 was bought for preservation at the end of the age of steam on British railways and can now be seen on the preserved Paignton and Dartmouth Steam Railway in Devon.

The reconstruction of Stockfield Road overbridge on 11 July 1939, with a GWR goods train approaching. Situated between Tyseley and Acock's Green on the GWR's main line to London, it was typical of a number of bridges in Birmingham which needed their arches widening to meet the demands of motor traffic.

Two such bridges existed in Aston Hall Road where the line out of Aston railway station forked westwards to Walsall and northwards to Sutton Coldfield. This was the scene shortly before work on them began in 1932 ...

... and on 1 May that year during reconstruction.

The completed bridges on 28 June 1933. Although the width of the new roadway in relation to the amount of traffic on it suggests a certain degree of overkill, the growth in motor vehicle use after the Second World War would soon prove otherwise.

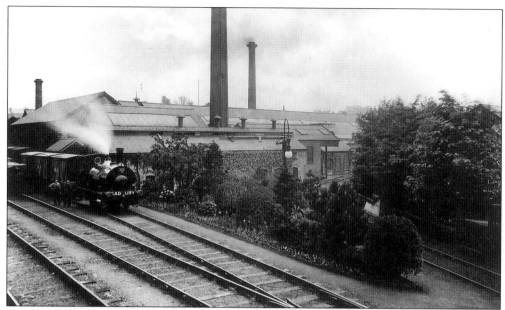

Many industrial complexes in Birmingham and the Black Country boasted their own internal rail systems, often with their own locomotives as well as wagons, and Cadbury's chocolate factory at Bournville was one of these. Here engine No. 2 (a Dick, Kerr 0-4-0 saddle tank, built around 1896) waits to proceed on its way. A large brass plate on each tank carried the name CADBURY.

Cadbury's first locomotive was an unnumbered Peckett 0-4-0 saddle tank of 1885 (Works No.440) bought that year. It is seen here on a train of company wagons sometime before it was sold to a Bloxwich contractor in 1894. Up to the time the system closed in May 1976 the railway had seen eleven steam and four diesel locomotives working it. Avonside 0-4-0 tank No. 1 in 1925 escaped scrapping and is now preserved at Birmingham Railway Museum at Tyseley.

Six
Motoring for the Masses

For better or worse, the motorcar has been with us for just over a century. Looking back, four dominant themes have manifested themselves during its history. Firstly, early cars were hand-built, produced in small numbers and were very expensive; consequently they were the preserve of the very rich. Secondly, after the First World War, mass production methods meant that there was a huge increase in the number of cars built at a greatly reduced unit cost, giving rise to widespread ownership. Thirdly, a spin off from this mass production was that small manufacturers amalgamated or were taken over, a process which led inexorably to the multinational giants of today. Finally, the dramatic growth in car use led to the wholesale remodelling of towns and cities as roads more suited to the horse and cart gave way to dual carriageways, flyovers and roundabouts. All these themes, in one way or another, are reflected in the following selection of photographs.

Herbert Austin, seated in an Austin 7 for a publicity shot, c. 1925. Production of this ground-breaking 'Chummy' began in 1922 and the company was selling 200 a week by the following year. Its 698 cc, four-cylinder engine produced 10 bhp. A saloon version first appeared in 1926.

Before the introduction of mass produced cars, like the Austin 7 or the Model T Ford, the market was dominated by rather more luxurious vehicles such as this early Rolls Royce, seen here with Mrs Muscott of Hay Mills and her chauffeur. Note the early Automobile Association badge on the bonnet.

Colmore Row on 8 July 1906. This was one of the decorated cars taking part in Joseph Chamberlain's 70th birthday celebrations.

The First World War was the first major conflict in which motorcars played a significant role, either behind the lines, on the battlefield or on the home front. An example is seen here at Soho railway station where the cars wait to convey wounded soldiers from the train to the hospital.

'Sitting cases' – patients who could sit upright – leaving Dudley Road Hospital for other hospitals in a similar convoy.

An aerial view of the Austin Motor Works at Longbridge seen from the south before the Second World War. The horseshoe-shaped housing estate, at the top of the photograph, was built by the Austin Motor Co. for its employees at the end of the First World War. In the bottom right is the company's private airfield.

Inside the works at Longbridge, *c.* 1930. A variety of bodies are being built on primitive assembly lines.

In total contrast, the works some thirty years on. This is the final assembly line for the Mini which was launched in 1959 when it was still known as the Austin Seven. The car was renamed the 'Mini' early in 1962. The bodies coming in overhead are being lowered onto the twin sub-frame chassis/engine units while in the background its immediate predecessor the A40 is being produced.

The Mini's big sister, the Austin 1100, coming off the production line and receiving the final touches before being driven away, c. 1963. This model was launched in August 1962, as the Morris 1100, with the Austin version appearing a year later.

Road widening on the Pershore Road in 1924. This was just one of many such schemes implemented between the wars as the Corporation endeavoured to cope with the demands of motorists and their organisations for better, wider, faster highways.

A busy crossroads, by 1939 standards. Here Yardley Wood Road crosses Wake Green Road with a wide variety of road users being controlled by the newfangled traffic lights.

Removing tram tracks from Birmingham's streets was a regular sight in the 1940s and '50s. Such work was usually carried out in conjunction with road improvement works as here in Bristol Street, with contractors Cox & Danks of Langley Green, *c.* 1952.

A decade on: the construction of the underpass at Six Ways, Aston, 1961. Such massive road widening schemes almost always meant the destruction of the buildings on one side of the original road, as was the case here. The block of shops on the left survives, however, though those beyond it do not.

Another great Birmingham car marque was that of Wolseley which actually began life as a sheep shearing company! However, at the end of the nineteenth century it turned to building cars designed by Herbert Austin. This was the works entrance in Drews Lane, Washwood Heath, c. 1934.

Assembling Wolseley Hornets at Drews Lane, c. 1934. This was a family saloon with a 1271 cc straight-six engine.

Assembling the two-door sports version of the Hornet, *c*. 1934. In 1905 the company was bought by Vickers, then later by William Morris and was transferred to Morris Motors in 1935.

Hornets receiving their final inspection at Drews Lane, *c*. 1934.

Dudley Road, Winson Green, with a typical garage of the period on 9 May 1960. In the pioneering days of motoring, oil and petrol were sold by chemists and repairs executed by the local blacksmith or cycle shop. As the number of cars on the road grew so the selling of fuel became a profitable business in its own right, as did servicing and repairs, and almost any old shop buildings were turned into workshops and had a petrol pump or two installed outside.

A similar garage in Harborne High Street, around 1960. Here, the existence of a small forecourt means that used cars can be displayed for sale.

Just yards away, a completely different type of garage exemplifies the modern approach, also around 1960. These were the spacious premises owned by one of the major petrol companies and were designed for as large and quick a through-put of cars as possible.

Redditch Road, King's Norton, on 2 March 1954: the blobby shape of things to come. With the end of rationing in the early 1950s came a rapid improvement in people's standard of living and a caravan in the front garden was, for many, a 'must have' status symbol.

Walsall Road flyover under construction at Perry Barr close to the Birchfield Harriers athletic track on 29 January 1971. The caravan and mobile home dealer's spacious premises provide ample proof that this aspect of British leisure was here to stay.

Seven
Commercial Haulage

Before the comparatively cheap motorcars of the inter-war years brought personal transport within the reach of many, few people would have made road journeys, other than by bus or tram, unless as part of their normal daily work. Apart from public transport vehicles, and the occasional cab or private carriage, almost all vehicles on the streets of Birmingham would have been earning their keep by carrying goods in to, out of, or around the city. Factories and shops had to be supplied, as did the large meat, flower and vegetable markets, hotels and inns and the hundred and one other commercial premises in the growing conurbation. In the nineteenth century this transport sector was served principally by the horse, just as it had been for centuries before, but the twentieth century saw an increasing dependence upon the internal combustion engine as vans and lorries became ever more powerful and reliable. There was by no means a sudden or clear cut transition from the one to the other though and in this selection – and indeed elsewhere in this compilation – the horse can be seen performing its faithful, age-old service long after the Second World War.

The High Street with a wide range of horse-drawn vehicles including a London & North Western Railway delivery wagon going about its daily business, c. 1903.

A typical farm wagon laden with straw on the weighbridge at Smithfield Market, *c.* 1895. The hardware shop in the background doubled as a modern bicycle works.

The old open air market in Moat Row in July 1896. Another farm cart laden with vegetables looms over a small, two-wheeled donkey cart.

Another two-wheeled cart, this time a much larger version employed during the demolition of Christ Church at the top of New Street in 1899. The view is towards Pinfold Street.

Two Italian ice cream sellers with their handcarts in the Bull Ring, *c.* 1898. A would-be 'man about town' is treating himself to an ice cream, while a delivery boy looks on enviously.

This milk cart, belonging to Red Hill's Dairy in Hay Mills, is little more than a step up in status from a handcart. It carries a single churn from which the driver would sell jugfulls of milk to the housewives along his daily route.

Redhill Road, King's Norton, *c*. 1930. A Ten Acres & Stirchley Co-op horse-drawn delivery van waits outside Gough & Thompson's general stores which was open from 1929 to 1932.

Erdington Laundry in Summer Road. The two large vans would have been used for collecting and delivering laundry in bulk from hotels and the like, while the wicker handcart would have been employed on a local domestic round.

A laundry van of similar design, this time from the Village Green Laundry at King's Norton.

As well as dairies and laundries, coal merchants and bakeries tended to use horse-drawn vans long after other tradesmen had made the switch to motor transport, probably because all three made leisurely rounds with frequent stops and starts. Here, a covered cart and a van stand outside H. Summers' Bakery on The Green, King's Norton, *c.* 1910.

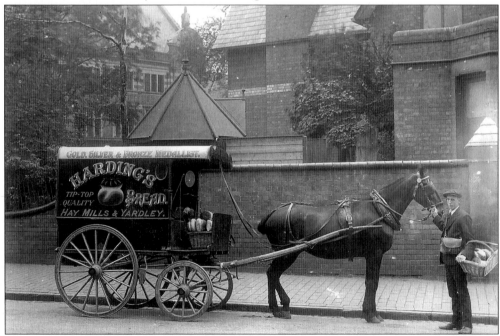

Mr George Bailey with his bread van which belonged to Harding's Royal Steam Bakery of Hay Mills and Yardley. The horse's name was Buller and the location was probably Byron Road in Small Heath, *c.* 1920.

A similar van, some ten years or so later, with a somewhat older George Bailey outside Mr Harding's house near the bakery in Coventry Road, Yardley. The van's number, No. 20, would suggest a sizeable delivery fleet.

A small, two-wheeled Selly Park Bakery van makes its unhurried way along Dad's Lane in Moseley in 1932. Only the roadside gas lamppost betrays the fact that this is an urban rather than a rural scene.

The premises of the Birmingham Battery & Metal Co. in Selly Oak in 1913. The line-up of cart horses and the two lorries would suggest that the photograph might well have been taken to mark the occasion of the replacement of the former by the latter.

Brewing was another trade which remained faithful to the horse long after most others had abandoned it. Indeed, some breweries still use them today for sound commercial as well as publicity reasons. Here, one of Ansell's drays is seen near the Aston brewery in 1951.

A motor van, possibly a Dennis, belonging to the wire rope manufacturers Latch & Batchelor Ltd of Hay Mills, probably about the time of the First World War. The proud driver's uniform is apparently heavily influenced by the uniform of the horse riding army officers of the period.

Another motor van. This one was a locally built Austin belonging to H. Johnson's 'Ideal' mattress factory in Bordesley Green, c. 1930.

An early, immaculately turned out motor hearse belonging to the Yardley Road firm of William Painter & Co., funeral directors.

A pair of Clayton & Shuttleworth steam wagons, FE1847 and FE2442, belonging to the haulage contractors Shephard & Hough of Stirchley. This is a reminder of a time when steam-powered vehicles were a common sight on the roads. This type of steam wagon was built in large numbers by this Lincoln based firm during the First World War when demand for them was high.

Eight
Flying High

The history of aviation in Birmingham goes back almost as far as that of heavier-than-air flight itself, one of the early landmarks being the founding of the Midland Aero Club in 1909. Immediately prior to the First World War, the playing fields at Castle Bromwich were used for flying demonstrations and then, when the war started, were requisitioned by the War Office and a military airfield built there. In 1919 it was licensed by the Air Ministry as a civil airfield and, in 1931, was brought within Birmingham's boundary. This selection of photographs concentrates on two aspects of Birmingham's aviation past: the construction of a new airport at Elmdon in the 1930s, to replace the one at Castle Bromwich, and the production of military aircraft at the older airfield during the Second World War.

In the nineteenth century hot air balloon flights were a great public spectacle and this ascent by a Mr Hudson at Cannon Hill in Edgbaston was no exception.

The ill-fated R-101 airship was photographed by a Hay Mills resident as it passed over the city on 18 October 1929. Built in 1929 by the Royal Airship Works at Cardington, Bedfordshire, it was intended to help develop transport within the Empire at a time when the concept of long-haul aircraft was not yet on the horizon. It was a truly massive machine, with a diameter of 131 ft, a length of 731 ft and a volume of almost 5 million cu. ft and was propelled by five Beardmore Tornado diesel engines developing a total of 585 hp. On 5 October 1930 it crashed just north of Paris while on a flight to India with the loss of 48 lives. The government then abandoned the idea of using such craft.

Once all airfields were like this: just an open field in the open air. This was the 800 acre Elmdon site of the new Birmingham airport on 9 December 1936.

Construction of the terminal building at Elmdon on 17 March 1938, shortly after work had begun. The proposal for a new airport had been approved by the city council two years before, after the Air Ministry indicated that Castle Bromwich would soon cease to cater for civil flights.

The same building on 19 July 1938, still set, apparently, in a sea of grassland.

By 21 October the final 'winged' form of the terminal building was clearly apparent and work was in hand on its immediate surroundings and neighbouring structures.

The terminal building, as seen from the shell of the new freight hangar close by, on 17 February 1939.

The terminal on 9 June 1939. Elmdon Airport opened for commercial operations on 1 May 1939 – although there was clearly much tidying up to be done before the official opening by the Duchess of Kent on 8 July!

Finished at last, after a total of £360,000 had been spent on the airport. This is the sight that would have greeted prospective passengers on 27 July 1939 as they were about to sample the novel delights of air travel.

On 9 May 1965, more than a quarter of a century on, the scene was remarkable similar, although inevitably it was busier and more cluttered – an indication of just how commonplace air travel had become.

The terminal in use in 1939. Parked on the apron in the foreground are a De Havilland 87B Hornet Moth (G-ADKV) and an 80A Puss Moth (G-AAZP), built by the same manufacturer. Both continued the naming tradition started by the more famous Tiger Moth.

Unloading a Douglas Commercial Dakota, the transport variant of the DC3, belonging to Aer Lingus at Elmdon in 1963. Well over 10,000 of these aircraft were built from 1935 onwards, many of which are still in service today.

A British European Airways' Vickers Viscount being readied for its next flight at the terminal in 1963, at a somewhat more leisurely pace than would be the case today. Viscounts began commercial flights in 1953 on the world's first propeller-turbine scheduled services. Production ceased in 1964, by which time 445 of them had been sold to over 60 operators in some 40 countries. Powered by four Rolls Royce engines, it had a range of nearly 1,500 miles and a top speed of 360 mph.

Elmdon airport buildings seen appropriately from the air in 1962. The scale of visible activity is a world away from that of the new terminal on the far side of the runways opened in 1984. The buildings are, from left to right: the terminal building, the freight hangar and one of the two larger aircraft hangars.

The airport, viewed from a slightly different perspective just five years later, with evidence of the remodelling of the main entrance and, to the far right, the future site of the new passenger terminal, Birmingham International railway station and the National Exhibition Centre.

At the start of Second World War Castle Bromwich was turned over to aircraft production. This is an overview of the factory late in the war when production was in full swing.

The main entrance to the factory in Kingsbury Road, *c.* 1943.

The main drawing office, *c.* 1943. Almost all the employees visible are men who would have been exempted from military service because of their special draughtsmanship skills which could not have been taught quickly to anybody else.

One of the Castle Bromwich tool rooms, *c.* 1943. Again, the workforce here is made up of men with years of engineering experience behind them who were employed to manufacture the machine tools needed to produce the various aircraft components.

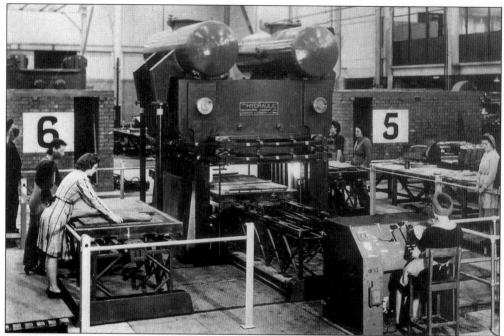

The press shop in F Block, around 1943. Here, the workers are women, drafted in and trained quickly to handle such semi-automated work as the pressing out of aircraft sections from metal sheets.

Women were also employed on many of the more laborious (and often disagreeable) tasks such as sealing the fabric coverings of petrol tanks in the dope shop ...

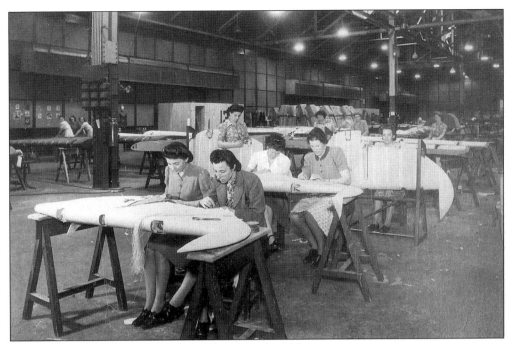

... or covering tail planes and fins with hand stitched fabric.

In late 1941 the production of Lancaster bombers began at Castle Bromwich. This is the fuselage assembly area of B Block, with the planes at an early stage of construction.

A row of nearly completed fuselages in B Block.

This was the first Lancaster completed at Castle Bromwich, registration HK535. It was tested at the factory on 22 October 1943, possibly the day this photograph was taken.

Spitfire production commenced at Castle Bromwich in 1940, the year before work began on the Lancasters. A similar construction pattern was followed: fuselages would first be assembled, each on its own trolley ...

... then they would be moved to a more spacious area for the wings and tail assemblies to be attached, along with the engines and undercarriages. They were then ready for the completing touches.

The finished result was a superb fighting machine such as this, registration RK869, one of a batch of 100 Spitfires completed in the late summer of 1944.

Castle Bromwich runway in the early summer of 1944 with Lancasters and Spitfires waiting to be dispatched to their designated squadrons. The airfield closed on 31 March 1958 and the 350 acre site was sold to the Corporation two years later and was used for the building of the Castle Vale housing estate.

Nine

Miscellanea

There now remain to be considered all those vehicles which, for one reason or another, do not fit easily into any of the preceding sections. Ranging from the humble handcart and perambulator, via the bicycle, to the vital but often neglected dust cart, they were delightfully enchanting or strictly utilitarian. Each in its own small way ensured that the life of the city went on, that the wheels did indeed keep turning.

The countryside comes to the city: a Ferguson tractor in Edmund Street, 1972, in the days before drivers' cabs were made compulsory. It is probably on Corporation business.

Edmund Street looking towards the Norwich Union building in 1904. There are a group of early bicyclists outside the demolition site of the Belle Vue Hotel. Also note the early garage sign just beyond.

Bicycle wheels being 'tuned-up' at the BSA factory on the Coventry Road in Small Heath. This job was traditionally performed by women as they were thought to have a defter touch than men.

A street scene in Aston in 1898. A group of urchins – one barefoot – are playing with a bamboo and iron baby cart.

A proud mother shows off her pram – and a member of the post-Second World War 'baby boom' generation.

A late eighteenth- or early nineteenth-century fire engine, with an appropriately costumed crew, taking part in Birmingham's 1897 Diamond Jubilee procession. The long bars either side of the machine would have been pumped up and down alternately to send a stream of water out of the top-mounted nozzle.

In complete contrast, the new fire station on Bristol Road South by the junction with South Road, Northfield, in 1960.

Selly Oak railway station during the First World War with trailers waiting to convey military 'stretcher cases' to hospital.

The last military out patients leaving Dudley Road Hospital by van and trailer.

A Birmingham firm of pneumatic engineers, Alldays & Onions Ltd, turned its expertise to the war effort, producing a wide range of medical vehicles at its Matchless Works in Fallows Road, Sparkbrook. They provide a chilling reminder of the carnage of those years. This simple handcart was used for moving 'stretcher cases' single-handed.

Alldays & Onions Ltd also designed a trailer for moving 'stretcher cases' by car. (See p. 119 for photographs of examples in use.)

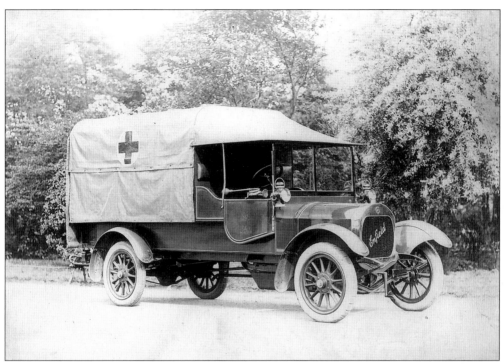

One of the company's ambulances which was basically a large open car fitted with a canvas roof.

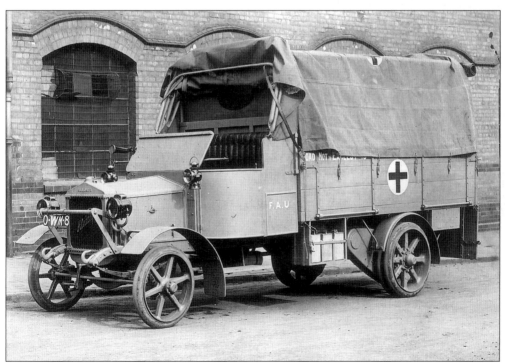

A larger ambulance, based on a lorry chassis this time.

Not all production was for the military though; Alldays & Onions also manufactured commercial vehicles such as this basic van.

A lorry belonging to Mills Munitions Ltd of Mill Street West, piled high with the firm's famous Mills Bombs. The Allied flags perched on top suggest that the occasion was an Armistice Day victory parade – and that the grenades were empty! Aston Science Park now covers the site of the factory.

A reminder of happier times before the war: Harborne High Street during the 1911 coronation celebrations, with the 'decorated bicycles' section of a parade passing by. Note the sign on the lamppost for the railway station.

The opening of West Heath fête, c. 1923. The fête was opened by Canon Price, vicar of King's Norton, who stood on the makeshift platform afforded by a cart belonging to Ernest Loxley, monumental mason of Northfield. In keeping with tradition, the audience finds it difficult to stay awake.

Some things never change: a float depicting 'The only beer well in the world' in the 1936 Birmingham University students' parade.

The circus comes to town. This Bertram Mills parade in the Coventry Road was organized to publicize a visit to Hay Mills in the early 1950s; a lorry-mounted human cannonball gun is to the fore.

The Detal Metal Co.'s Delta Works in Dartmouth Street in the 1920s or '30s. There are at least ten of the firm's open lorries to be seen here, fitted with temporary seats for a works' outing for employees' children.

A horse-drawn ash wagon or dust cart being connected to the 'chain-horse' at the Montague Street depot just east of the city centre, c. 1930. The chain was used to help the wagon up the incline to the refuse hoppers. However, it fell out of use during the 1930s when the use of horses was discontinued.

Hauling logs at an unknown location. These road locomotives were once a common sight before diesel tractors powerful enough to perform such tasks were produced. The name of this engine would suggest that it was built in 1911, the year of the coronation of King George V.

An Invicta steamroller in Berkeley Road, Hay Mills, probably in the 1930s. The workmen are holding the tools of their road surfacing trade, notably rakes and shovels.

A Book Exchange Service van belonging to Birmingham Public Libraries, outside the old Central Library in 1929.

Another Corporation vehicle of similar vintage, this time a general runabout belonging to the Baths Department, equally immaculately turned out.

The last tramcar in Birmingham, No. 616 again (see p. 68), in Miller Street on 4 July 1953. Was this the end for Birmingham's trams? Not quite! Nearly half a century on, they are running once more, this time on the new Midland Metro (opened 1999) to West Bromwich and Wolverhampton. The city's remarkable transport history has entered yet another era.